THE WATERMELON AND OTHER POEMS

RAJAT DUTTA

INDIA • SINGAPORE • MALAYSIA

ISBN 979-8-89186-555-6

Contents

Going Home After the Day's Work

What is pressing is the immense positivity
Boxed in your frame. I see it every time
You walk away.

With that thought, I walk
Towards the bridge that
Will sweep us all inside the crowded Metro.
We are now in an
Air-conditioned auditorium
Where Yo-Yo-Ma has

Just started the Bach Cello suit in G major.
And in a parallel universe
You and I are still singing in the rain.

While the tired day is returning home.

Attachment

You are not going out
To perform your daily outdoor work.
This is not only my knowing
But also the dictation presented
By the sheet of dust
So shamelessly attracted to your
New grey synthetic leather boots.
If only they know, maybe tomorrow
Or, for the matter of fact, right now
You might dust them off.
I wish to share the reality.
Then I remembered that
Youtube video you forwarded last
Tuesday. On self-realisation.

What Is It

That you want me a certain way
And I want you to be someone else.
The fight is not to accept this.
Yes, there are undeniable feelings
Love and hate.
But my solitude and your anxiety
They just don't want to be friends.

From That Day

The first thing I remember it rained
The next thing I remember is you
Sitting there.
I guess the lobby
It was, and they were repainting
A section of the wall as it was not
Agreeing with the brand colours.
It was no love at first sight.
But something in your eyes.
I am yet to solve it, my dear.

Another spring poem

Listen ——————————————
If winter was that canvas
You bought along with that
Silver-coloured rice cooker as
Shipping was free

And summer was that fight
We had to figure out where
To hang the sunflower portrait
You drew

Then the time we knitted together
In between was spring

Lighthouse Hill

You know the drill
To stand tall and guide us all
I wonder who lives in you
To turn the light
In the darkest of nights.

If you ever miss your home
Just let me know
And I will take you back
To the one you love
And the one who
Loves you.

On a Date with a Poem

The title came in through the revolving door
With an open bayonet, much like pictures, I have
Seen from the Great War.

The rest of her she dragged
To eat up the allotted time. As if trying to slaughter
The introduction and head towards the main course table.
Finally, we settled, and customary drinks were served.

With a sheepish smile, the waiter judged my probable
Chance with her. She started verse one by defining
Acceptable rational behaviour. When it ended, I searched.
For the appropriate smile. But I failed and presented my case.
With a meaningless 'wow'. Which, by the way she hated.

Then came questions, not with dreamy, mischievous, flirting
eyes
But with unclad reasoning about life.

I was lost, trying to find the answer to the question:
'Are her eyes really that brown
or is it the lighting?'

When the final verse came, I had given up the battle. Then she said,

'It's late, and for us to meet again, we must reach home safe. Will text

You once I reach, please text me back too'.

Knowing Myself

The first act was to judge everyone
And who would have thought
A hedge flower will be the one
To hold the mirror for me to look at

So, I wish you good
The one I hate
The one who hates me
The one I love
And the one who can't love me back

Act two was to judge myself
And who would have thought
A disabled dog will be the one
To hold the mirror for me to look at

So, I wish me good
And a treat for the road ahead

The final act, and I am sorry to declare
Have not prepared it yet.

On the Beach

Like every day, I swallowed the salt,
I smeared my face with a sulfur smell
Of bacteria digesting dead plankton.
I walked around and built a sand castle.
Today, I see anxiety in your eyes
Almost ready with words in your mouth,
Though you are conscious not to
Break the world suddenly.
Dear Sea, today you are like soldiers
Coming home with every wave,
After the war has been declared over.

Bed Sheet of Justice

The new bed sheet we bought
From IKEA last weekend
Here you are putting the bed sheet
As I stand patiently by the floor lamp thinking
Is this bed sheet
Black on white
Or white on black
Or mixed equally
Without discrimination
Tonight, let us sleep on justified land

Every Day Love

After losing the battle
I can still go
To find a suitable place
For you to keep your dreams

This love is

A sailor's biography
About survival at sea
It is a seasonal flower
In the valley of unsung angles

It is every day
I love you like an April bath
It is every day
I love you like a December shawl

Streetlights

Ok. So, you are leaving?
I know you know the way
And whatever unknown
You will fathom immaculately.
Let me come along
May not be the guiding star
But the street lights.
It's still dark out there.

Freedom

While tracing the shadow
Of the flying eagle
Over the material world,
I realised.
This antique soul
Of mine is
In love with your freedom.

A Line from Your Poem

I see unclad freedom
Staring back at me.

The one I read yesterday
Was trespassing hope
In the middle of a holocaust.

And the one I am reading
Is finding a home
In a town, dropped after the recession.

Then there was that one
Where love song is
The scattered sweet smell of elm.

A line from your poem is life.

To the Mother

In your creative belly
You hooked the fragile me
On a string among many.
Situations like burning clouds
Pouring down to hurt me
Is the game,
And you defeated them
Always.
You define, what strength is.

Poetic Inspiration

I am looking for a poem.
As if trying to find your eyes
Among the known and unknown.

I visited Collins.
Then I dragged myself out of Ezra,
Only to find myself swimming
Along the shores of Carlos.

From Sand Creek Ortiz called,
Followed his trail to find myself
Walking back home with Silas.
Till the end of the hired man.

Some days I cry, but not today.
This day is to seek a poem.
Outside the vanishing sunset,
The white lights switching on
And darkness is arriving.

Ginsberg said Krishna and
I took my flight back to India.
To my very own Joyda.

If I am not going to get her tonight,
Will close the diary and walk up to the bed.
While the dog barks in triplets,
Sleep sleepless dream dilemma
Maybe just an image of her
Will do tonight.

Varanasi

Smeared in ash, the river
Adjacent to the ghat
Looks like Shiva from
One of the calendars
We used to have it in our home.
The bed sheets and the towels
On the opposite bank
Do they belong to Parvati?
Varanasi, the city
Where tourists, pilgrims, and death
Breakfast together
Kachori, Rabdi
And the unending chanting
'Har Har Mahadev'.

The Us will it Remain

You and I
We are changing like the seasons
When our dead skin meet again
After time has passed from
The bottle to the melamine bowl
On a windy morning
Outdoor, by the breakfast table
Placed next to the rhododendron tree

Will they talk about the
Initial days or about
That time when we were
Distancing each other to avoid eye contact
And what about history?
Will it behold us?

Your Name

If I take your name now
In this room, it will become public.

Common friends will ask
Why, how, when, what happened, and why not resolve it?

And my resolve to not
Let your peace distort
Could not be saved.

Instead, I will pour your name
For myself. Slowly, one alphabet
At a time. Then, at the window
While everyone is running
Away from the evening rain
I will take my first sip.

Almost Summer

After 300 jumbled-up words
And 30 slaughtered more of
Pimped allegories.
There is nothing to write today.
The afternoon air is getting
Warm every day
Summer is here.

Momos and Chopsticks

Don't know
Don't know if this poem
Will knock on your door.
Some mornings, while I eat breakfast and
Listen to the neighbours dog barking
I wish it did.

This is about momos.
I order momos from a place you don't know
They slip a pair of chopsticks wrapped
In a napkin printed zhù nǐ hǎo yùn

I don't know what that means
And I have decided not to google

I tried to use the chopsticks
the way you taught me.
I failed, and the momo

I was experimenting with
Erupted on the napkin
Exposing spinach and cheese.
As if Mount Vesuvius has decided
To bury Pompeii again.

Portrait

This is an evening sickness
When I feel like I am the sea.
Without any start
Or even an end.
Hanging there.
Like the perfectly balanced portrait
Of a fruit basket, hanging on
The 5th floor conference hall.

Tonight, the Sun is Bright

Poetry, much of it is written
Inside a room
When the day is getting doomed.
Or the night is in bloom.
At odd hours, when you should be
Mailing that important presentation
Or maybe get the groceries.
And also on Sunday afternoons.

And if you ask me to describe that line,
'Tonight the sun is bright'

I don't know.
It was around 8:45 p.m.
She came home after office
I was sitting there and wrote:

Tonight, the sun is bright.

Cherry Blossom Season

If you would have told me
I would have dressed up.
In the colour of the ocean,
Tattooed some mountains,
The fleeting beauty of cherry blossoms
And smeared the smell of fallen leaves.
If there are any.

You have caught me off guard
These are daunting times.
Words are misleading
Dying petals of seasonal flowers.
Thoughts are soldiers
Marching towards your will.

Let this moment flow
Don't think of anything
Just look at each other.
And tomorrow, we can issue
A formal invitation
To come to the party
Like we want.

Dream

Your hair, I dream
The way you play with them
Change colours like seasons
How rebellious they are
How obedient they are
One day, like the river
One day, like a waterfall
Some days intentionally
I go missing in them.
Wishing when I come back

I can only find you.

Sunset

Azure affirmation
With welcoming
Orange lining.
Golden impression of
The distant sun.

You swallow me,
I let it be.

Many Moons Ago

We walked side by side.
Under the silver sky
With promises in our hearts.

Like climbers, our hands
Resting on each other.
I asked, and your eyes
Pearl black with powdered brown crystals
Said Avanti.

For my fingers to trace
The green river flowing
Underneath your skin,

As I stood there beside you
Tracing the river made out of
History and the lineage that has

Given this world a life to recreate itself.
I wondered from where
You have got those eyes filled with

The depth of a black hole
The vastness of the sea
And then there is this light

Stolen from some uncharted galaxy.
This was many moons ago.

Zindagi

Uchi inch geliyon se
Guzarti zindagi
Khatti meethi
Chashni se behti ye nadi

Rota hain kahi ye dil
Kahi mile khushi
Paani ka rang namkeen
Chaat mai milale yahi

Jab tak mile
Puri jeele zindagi

Rain

It's been raining.

For how long, I lost track of it
Past 1:10 last night.

The shivering street called my name
And as I looked out the bedside window,
The plants outside
Looked drenched too.

I woke up before the alarm hit the
Snare at 6 a.m.

To wake you up.

'Please go get some cups
While I turn on the stove,
And take the milk out of the refrigerator.

"Why so early?" You asked

'Because we are having tea with friends'.

The Watermelon

The gloom of this afternoon
Reverberated by slanting rain
And the howl of the ganging winds

As you decide to revolt
I decided to cut the watermelon
Today, not tomorrow

The luscious red is like
Meditation: calm and silent
The way your phone is

When the do not disturb
Button is On
And allowed notifications
From people and apps are none.

Three Sparrows Fighting

I sailed from my writing chair,
Crossing the sea
Of white tiles and docked
On the side of the bed, just now.

From here, I can see my table
Standing silently,
A lighthouse
On a faraway island
In its own world.

From the table, I moved
To the faded brown window,
Three sparrows are fighting
Over things in their lives
Which I will never get
Much like the intricate science of existence.

Then they left, one
Then two together

And I am left with a
Thought. I will probably
Never see them again
And so many others.

Black Water

Black water glistened with
Periodic lights white and yellow.
Waves, they look like snake skin
Swimming away, swimming in, are calling.
The lovers call to annihilate you before
The world gets you.

What will the impression be
When you hit the water?

It will be remorseful
When anguish breaks the
Silence of the sea.

Walk

Let's take a walk

To cut the vagueness in the air and
To box the undulating feelings.

Let's talk about that dream of yours

There used to be a river and
Boats, you said.

Yes I did
But you know what

The water has now dried up
In patches.
Boats are benches engraved with names
From a past memory.

Come, it's about to rain
Let's go back home.

Death by Hanging

John, they hanged you
In August 1692, in Salem, Massachusetts.

And here I am sitting
On another August of 2023
Somewhere 8000 miles away.

Scrolling through pictures
When I saw your tombstone,
I googled you.

And I went through the Wikipedia page
To read about your
Third wife, your accuser
And the outcome of the trial.

Then came the aftermath
And the Crucible by Arthur Miller
Sitting here I think

What was going through you
When they hanged you
And after.

But by then you may
Have been elevated and cared for
None, of what
They did down here.

Tenerife, Canary Island, Spain

Never been there.
But I see you now
A picture of you.

The royal blue sea in your backyard
The golden sun shining on the
The white walls of the small house
With a bell and a stop sign

Hanging on a post just outside.
I see people and their skin
Patinaed as they go
Basking in the sun.
I see a couple of red crabs
Resting on the decayed rocks.

Cables, they run freely
From home to home
Casting shadows on white walls.
A window with white curtains

Facing the sea.
There is no one standing there
I imagined, on certain days
Someone does at sunset
Facing the sea.

Thinking about a lost love, or
A distant place in the mountains, or
The plains, or maybe snow.

A Lost Poem

Then I was writing about March

How the moisture in
The air is sweltering
The salt from the sea
Is cutting your lips

There was a line about the sun too

Now I stand in July
searching for her
I have lost the poem.

Ricochet

One of your poems starts with a Ricochet

Where you are catching a train
To go missing from this known city of ours
As I reread that poem of yours

I can see the streets
Running to your house with a green door
Calling your name
Asking you not to rebound from what is here.

But you always believed in
What is waiting for you.
I see your pen and the

The second hand of the table clock
Which was a gift moving
As your lines ricocheted off a nearby park
Then move away, far away to places

I can only think of.
You are here now.

Including new characters
In your new play in
A new city and pressing
All the values in time.

The Gift of Silence

Is what our Father gave us.

In our years of living together
In one house and then another.

We hardly spoke.
What I remember the most
Is his way of making evening tea

Imitating the pensive silence of dawn.
From him I learned, it is not necessary
To throw words

To ripple the silence of life.
Maybe there is a world where
People speak the language of eyes.

Now that he is gone and
After so many years
It came to me as a fleeting thought.

We were strangers
Sharing the same home.

Aimlessly

As I walked aimlessly
Circling the city
It was not ambitious
Of me to ruffle the

Memories of a sunken ship
The one not made out of steel or wood
But of other things
How long will you

Stay
Asked the promenade
Anchored in the lee of her smile

Maybe until the traffic
Turns green

And then on
A new street
We walk on

Cold Latte

Everything was perfect
When she came.
The ice floating on the top

Like the divider wall
Between you and me.
The rest of it was

An artists expression
Of mixing colours.
White, cool ash

Deep brown and a hint of gold.
It was me who
Jumbled it up,

Killing the art.
Like a sudden storm
After days of summer

When dust gets into
Your eyes
And you cry.

I took the straw
Plunged it into the mixed
Emotions of cold latte.

By then battle
Judge and jury
Everyone has gathered

In my throat.
The taste went away,
What I was left with

Was immense coldness.
The one we feel
For each other these days.

Udashi

She let me in
Made me grow
Without even knowing

I loved her
And as I was getting
Ready to accept her

To pin me down
She left behind
Ashes just a reminder she was here

How do you write your poems?

Is the question that intrigues me
More than your poems
Is there any ritual you follow?
A specific time of the day or night
What about pens?
Or have you completely
Moulded yourself into a
Screen and keyword setup?
Do you have a favourite chair?
A "can't-write-without" window?
Or is it
Poems they just come
And sit on your balcony
You pick them one after another
As per your mood for that day
And place them in your books
Accordingly.

A New Word

I went to bed with the same delusion
The one with which I've been living these days.

It will work out between you and me one day.
In the morning I took my delusion on a walk
To the east end park.

It was heavy on its feet.
So we sat on the bench by the pond.
It was then I saw a post by you

Talking something about delulu.
I looked up delulu to find out
There is a delusion

Living in your head too.
I looked in the eye of my delusion
And let the leash go.

Drying Clothes

You see, nothing will dry up.

The clouds have no place
But the sky above you and me.

When it's time to go,
I will leave behind
So many of these clothes.

Keep them in your almirah.
Keep them for the longest period
Till time cuts in to rob them of my smell.
And once I am gone
You should give them away.

Don't hold them close.
I am dead now.
Even better, cut the black jeans
And make a door mat.

I will know where I lay
Even when I am not there.

Sky

I woke up in the morning
And felt like "I am the sky"
All of you who came, left, and stayed
You are clouds.

But then I know how easy it is
To say all of that
Much like opening the fridge
To get the juice bottle.

Deleted All

I deleted all of it
The pictures and the texts
Now they live in me

The paper on which
There lived a poem on how you made me feel
Is darkened grey

Every day, I woke up thinking
"Today I will delete you."
And I find myself in a dark place

There is a giant screen
Running a silent movie of images
Then the day dies in the arms of the night

And you turn out
To be the unfinished poem
With whom I go to bed

Not to sleep
But to delete myself
Bit by bit

Lyrics to that Song

I shared a song with you
The one talking about where
We are heading to

I saw me in the lyrics
Walking the forest alone while it's raining.
I wanted you to see you
Whichever way you end up

When this ends too.
I kept walking into the heart
Of the forest. Lost completely
Still want to be lost

There I saw a mountain
It's peak shining
Shining with your tears or smile.
By then it was too dark
To figure out.

The forest is bleeding
It is making me numb.
The same numbness this song brought
The one that I shared with you.

No One to Save Me Tonight

How long can you burry
What is meant to hurt
Under the sheets

I have been doing so
Since last Monday here
We sailed on to a new port
On a Sunday

The night is here
Silent, staring back at me
Like newborn babies do

I can see from the dark side of the sheet
All those raging faces
I have been burring

I can't sleep now
Captain, let's go, this shore
Is not for us no more

Dead Flowers

The book of flowers
Lay dead now
On a concrete bed

First, a neon bicycle stamped
The Lavender
Who was already bedridden

And you were so busy
Explaining why we
Should end this

You never noticed your
Heels digging deep in
The Heart of the Dahlia

Introduction

Hi! Hello! Over here

I just came in yesterday
You must have noticed
You see I can't bear
Silence for long

Yesterday when my grandson
Gave me the first morsel
Of sweet earth

I saw you staring at me
From your window
You remember this is how
It was decades ago

Before partition came
And decided our fate
But then there were people

And I didn't want to
Make things awkward
We never got an introduction

I am Faiz and before
This lying down and waiting
I used to be a poet

A Slow Afternoon

Falling flowers make no noise
They just go. You see massive humility.
Much like you, a slow afternoon.

When I was doing the dishes
I saw you through the glass window.
Playing silently with your friends.

And here I am making tea,
While pouring milk
As I glanced out
Of the same glass window
You are gone.

Your friends are still waiting
For you in silence.

Will You Hate me?

It came in like it always does.
That day, when we stood
Facing the sunset. Watching passerby
With battle scars and love in their eyes
Pain burdening them with
A slouch as they walk.

Will you hate me
If I go back?

Everything conspired against us
To bring us to where we stand.
Even when I forced those fidgety
Moments in my heart,
I knew that I was trying
To love an era that is gone.

You are a mirage
Never really there.
And I am searching for
Days, months, years, or more.

The convolution made me
Run for the experience
A sight in my dreams
Never really there.

Blame Who

Deliberately wasted lives
Deliberately wasted lines

Words forced almost chocked to
Fall in one after another.
That doesn't mean they
Love sitting next to each other.

Why write when there is no flow?
Not a stream of conscious effort.
Subdued, like those
Speechless nights. When you
Have things to say, but
No words no one to listen to.

Who is to be questioned?
Blame who? Me, you, poetry
I better get up,
Get going. It is dark outside
Now it is easy to hide.

Birthday

I know where you live.
But I don't know how you are.
I remember your face, but I
Don't know which face you are making now.

Is it that patented smile
With an indent on your left cheek, or is it
The stressing one with flickering eyes?

I know where you work
But I don't know
What you do after work these days.

I know three days from now
Is your birthday.
And I know I can't wish you
Happy birthday.

By trying to say it in your mother tongue
Only to falter along the lines
And you will gracefully erase the faults
To take the me as I am.

I know, I will not be able to plan
A surprise birthday party for you.
It is too late and
The sun is already shining.

Sunset 1.1

This is not the first time,
I have seen you earlier,
Like falling in love.

Stumbling face down first
Splashing reasons here and there.

But now there is more
Understanding in my blood.
That's what I tell myself
After taking online courses
On mental wellbeing and letting go.

I know
You the sun of today
Will have to go.
Tomorrow you may come. Come, clouds.
Whoever comes, I will again pour love

And if you are still not convinced,
It is upon your judgement
To do what you feel like.

A Picture Where Everyone Looked Happy

As I lay on my stomach
With my left elbow
Digging deep into the blue bed sheet
All of you look so happy

Unknown people in this unknown picture.
I know, individually, each one of
You must have so many troubles.
There is always a gatekeeper

Not letting you in the
World where you want to be.
But in this picture,
All of you have decided

Not to face him.
Instead, you stand, looking ahead
And behind you stand
Huge murals of cedars

And sunlight like little tassels.
It is good to see you
Look happy, not getting carried away
By what is waiting on the

Another side of one tick of the clock.

A Poem Beyond the Realm of You and Me

After the summer, before the snow
There will be a plot, a picture, or a luncheon.

With scores of characters
Signing up the lawns
Drawing attention to the

Grand drawing room.
There will be non of my feelings or
Your diction. Nothing about the table lamp

Obviously no mention of sunsets.
Just the characters running, loving,
Fighting, hiding, dying

Or even premature labour.
But we will not be in the vicinity
Of the lawn or the house.

We are in a restaurant
Eating bao and deciding
What will it be for the main course?

Farmers Market

On Sundays, do you
Get to choose your spot?
Dear, vegetable cart,

Sometimes, while I am bored
To look at the same vegetables
And they are equally bored
Staring at me.

I play a game, a game
Where I pretend not to know
Their name and only identify
Them by colours.

If you follow the rules
Of the game, you will find
Yourself standing in a
Busy art exhibition
On a Sunday.

Snowfall in Your City

We always call when it's
Sunday here and a late Saturday
In your city.

When I called
You started with "You just
Missed the snowfall".

How come I miss something
I don't even know of.
Yes, I have a list of things
That I miss doing.
And I am yet to add
Snowfall to that list.

Now that I see your city
Standing behind you
I find the snow to be encroaching.

Your city to me is a white ocean
Your city to me is a white forest
Your city to me is a white desert

And I kept thinking
What on earth I am doing here
When I should be there with you
Before the snow
Gets you completely.

One Breath at a Time

Look around, there are
So many unfinished
Poems hanging at this hour
When it is not even a complete day
Not even a complete night.

And Billy Collins is an optimist
To think of finding three great ones
In this lifetime.
When I can do with one at least.

Now is the battle within
Where you can let the opponent win
Or decide not to fight.

I decided to be an optimist too
And deal with this situation
One breath at a time.

The Trigger

When he pulled the trigger
He never realised that
A ghost will be waiting for him from now.

The nights get darker
He smells blood in the air
A child sleeps in his room
Silently, and leaves every morning
Without saying goodbye.
The walls are soaked with tears
Of a widow and a blind mother.

He is scared to look, scared
When someone calls his name
Down the street.
All of it seems to be the sound, the sound of a
Body hitting the ground.

The body hit the ground
And left a big hole
In his stomach.

The Life of You

The walls of this house are crumbling
Much like your skin. Ageing has come
For you, your way of life.
The dried water marks I have been
Noticing them closely, they look like you.
The wooden house that houses your gods,
Old idols, older wood is rotting on the edges.
Your gods, too, live like you do.
While you slept, I was going through every
Piece of material in this house.
Now I can say you are not materialistic.
I was standing next to your bed. You asleep
Breathing in and breathing out.
Even your eyes, they looked tired
Of everything they have been through.
I see a garden dead now. There once
Lived all your wants, but it is you who
Has killed them, buried them there, and
Have set the place on fire.
For your supplies, you look at us
For a new saree, you want us to

Look at you. We are travellers waiting
On the same bus stop, boarding the
Same bus. But there is a distance between us.
A circle, and we live our lives in tangents.
The refrigerator in this house is mint green, which is older than me
Was initially white. Opening the door, I saw
Our lives are frozen in there, resting on shelves.
Distracted, much like veins on your hands.
Evenings you sip tea and watch TV
The pixels run so deep, it is hard to see the
Faces on the screen. Dissolving slowly
The way your life is. Later that day,
I took a flight to fly back to where I live
Looking down, I see you waving and our town
Waving too. All of you are crumbling
Flowers after prime, not fallen, but life is
Lost. And from here, I see you
Looking up and smiling with a sad face
While I take you with me in my heart.

New love

You stayed for days with me, which I loved.
Most of that love is in a grave now
With an emerald tombstone.

Now I love another
In the darkest of nights
I find your eyes still searching
Someone must be loving
Them tonight.

You stayed for days with me, which you loved.
I don't judge; I have seen
Remorse crawling up my body
Then shivered with the pain of loss.

I stayed with them; I never ran.
To seek your love that is gone
I never hated what I felt
I stayed with them; I never ran.

There is no new canvas
The flesh is old and bones.
Imprinted with the love you left.
To be styled by new love.

This is How Mother Described Father Died

It was much into the
Darkest hours, when silence of death
Ambiguously mixed with the
Silence of the night.

He woke up and shivered once
Prayed and then went back to sleep.
To sleep, slumbering away from
My mother and us.

There was no drama, only every
Atom in his body bowed to the
Coming of death and followed.
Even while he was going

He maintained the silence
With which he
Lived his life.

These Days

These days, I pack as many
Poems as I can then lock
The door and leave.

Poems, some stay
Others fall, they go
I don't go behind them
To look for. I don't go
Your way to look either.

It is that I am tired, tired, tired.
To do any of the things
I should have. It feels like

A night's sleep will heal
The hollow in me
But one sleep is never enough.

I wake up in the middle of the day
Eat some more poems
With some more rum.

The bottle I have been
Keeping these days.
So I can laugh, laugh

At and with me;
Your laugh I still can't laugh like that.

We Live

I know you
I know them;

Everyone burning emotions
Like they burn leaves of winter, fallen dead,
Then will come some more;

Like uninvited greens of monsoon
They know they have to die
And with them will die
That smile you exchanged
When you walked past them
In the corridor

That one kiss
And none after that
It is hard

Since you and I are not clouds
Meant to let go
We live with belongings

But then you have to
you know
All of this life is

Piled up feelings in time
And we have to be moving
My heart aches

My pen is heavy
Dear beloved, we loved but then.

On a Saturday

I have noticed they usher
A rebel in my body
The moment I woke up.

A sickening burning motion
Of grudging like a forest fire
Slowly reaching the nearing

Town. All the animals they
Have already left or dead.
We are also preparing to run.

While the morning moves
With her shaky hands
From being a chain smoker

Her one-sided lover the
Afternoon is still hanging
There with hope.

The last orange fibre
Of the dying day
Is good enough to

Rehearse for the dark
Moments. When the stars
To guide me to bed

Have all fallen into the river.

The Death of February

I rushed to the window
But she smashed her
Own frame to let me know

The storm has arrived
From the west
I am holding on to my strength

To let her out
She is all set with
Her cavalry to tear
The room down
Here we stand
Your pictures scattered
By the February storm

Me looking at them
And in front of us
Stands the white wall

With a window built in 1914

The Name will be Lost

You died on a Sunday
All I wanted is to tell you
I am an ardent fan
Who bunks a bed
Somewhere in your city

It's been so long
That I don't remember
Since when I started adoring your voice

It is your voice that helped me
To feel love the way I
Feel it now;
It is your voice that
Helped me cry freely;

On Monday, I listened
To that song of yours,
Where you beautifully put
The fact, that one day
All our names will be lost,

And I missed something
Bigger in my heart.

Then I went out to walk
By the sea and heard that
Song of yours
Where lovers call for their love
Hoping the sea will
Address their call.

Then I started to flow back
From sand onto the concrete
And back home
But you know,
It doesn't matter.
You will only end for me
When I hit the ground.

Why Not Now

Why am I holding on,
When I know it is here
Just so it can go?

Why not now take
All the poems I can and
Run, run to an unknown

City and hide behind
The dirty mirror of
Some shady bar.

I know you will never
Come to search for me,
But at least if you do

The lost me will be hard
For you to find.
Why not now, I am

Letting the fear of
Losing drench me.
Diseased lying on a bed,

Knowing that the world
Is going on the way it plans
Why not now, I am

Cutting the cord and letting
Myself fall down
The Abbys and while

I fall, I try hard to avoid
Hearing you smile and
Focus on all the dead poets speaking.

Why not now
Why not now
Let the end hit.

The end of the road
Then I can go back to
Living a life unknown.

The Emptiness

Come closer you will see it in me

The waves of fear roaring in my heart;
The drumming of a sad rumble
Eating my stomach.

I slept and slept some more
The bed is my grave
Finally hugging me the way
I want to be hugged.

It is day again
Drop me off this ride;
Let me get the next train
Out of this petty land of emptiness.

A Picture of You

[We are far away now and I am yet to figure out the distance]

I saw a picture of you
Sitting among mountains;
You always believed
They are your friends.

You are facing the sun, smiling.

In that picture, lives a mountain river
And an iron bridge
I barely noticed the first time.

Your face is shining
As if the seasons are changing
And it's time for the melting of ice.

In the evening I went back
And looked again. I focused
On your eyes

And felt a cold stream
Flowing away from
Where they say the

Human heart is located.

Texting Battle

I was wondering if Sun Tau
Has any documented literature
On texting battles.

As I have been losing
After relentless attempts
To put forward my objectives on your screen.

After every bout
I go back to check
What went wrong
And every time I

Find my proposed content
Out of context
And not what I meant.

As if someone has placed
A giant banyan tree in the
Middle of a football ground.

Every time you take a leap
To reach the goal
The ball gets tangled.

Madh Fort

The sun fell at your feet and
Got drowned in the sea. We crossed
The water on a white boat to
Visit Madh Fort. That going to me
Felt like, we were one now, free from
The haunting of reality. The sea,
Its waves and salt made me sad.
I hold your hand tighter, you were
Looking ahead, I was looking at
You, knowing this will go soon.
When we reached the fort
It was closed. So we hiked
Up a hill for a better view.
It was there I took some
Pictures of you for me to keep.
The humidity was not rational,
It bothered us. So what? we kissed
And I wiped the tears off
Your eyes and sweat off your forehead,
To make way for another kiss.
We stood there, looking at life

Passing by, calling us. But time
Was running out and we had to
Leave Madh Fort and each other.
We took the boat back, this time
You standing beside me holding
My hand for support.
Was it not firm enough,
Why did you have to go?

They Killed a Mountain

They killed a mountain
To make way for an airstrip.
The debris, they have been

Piled up by the roadside
In the shape of another mountain.
But this one looks dead;

Shrunken, pale. As I drove
Past the dead body, the
Mountain within looked at me.

I was not bold enough
To say a thing. There was
Nothing I could have done.

But the mountain spoke
"I know you have no power
Over others. But what about you?

Why push yourself to oblivion,

Death is coming,
You must learn to live,

Like I did.
Before they decided
To kill me."

www.ingramcontent.com/pod-product-compliance
Lightning Source LLC
La Vergne TN
LVHW091113150826
845673LV00002B/806